THE FEELING

OF JAZZ

Text by
GEORGE T. SIMON

Drawings by Tracy Sugarman

SIMON AND SCHUSTER · 1961

Contents

Introduction

The feeling of jazz is something very personal. It means many things to the many people who live in its world. For some it is entirely pure, raw emotion; for others it is primarily stark, intellectual realism. To some it means happiness; to others sorrow. Because of it some grow rich, while others wallow in misery. But on one thing all agree: jazz is a way of making music, a means of expression, a highly personalized musical message of self-expression.

During the years I have been close to jazz, I have listened to many of its musicians—listened not only to their music but also to their words. They have told me how they feel about their lives of jazz: about what they play; about how they work and why they work; about all the conditions under which they exist; about the way they are treated; about their ambitions and disappointments; about their loves and their hates; about their relationships with other musicians, with their families, with their friends, with audiences, agents, producers, and with the many others who affect their music and their lives.

In this book I have attempted to express many of these feelings through the words of fictitious characters, but all based upon mixtures of real people I have known. It is, I guess, more a series of personal reports—reports from the inside out, rather than the usual historical surveys or analytical appraisals of jazz written (often quite effectively) by outsiders looking in. And it is my hope that after having read these pieces you will gain a truer understanding of the music and the people who have created it.

If you do, of course, much of the credit goes to Tracy Sugarman, whose sensitive drawings have captured so well graphically what I have tried to express verbally. I am intensely grateful for his contributions and also for having had the chance to work with and really know such a wonderful person. The same thing goes for our editor, Dick Grossman, who, fortunately, like Tracy, possesses an innate love of jazz.

And my final batch of thanks goes to Bev, Julie and Tommy, whom I love very much, and who seemed to understand that I would return in my original form whenever I left them to hunch over my typewriter to become any one of the number of characters whose loves and hates and joys and frustrations and other intense emotions have contributed to the feeling of jazz.

GEORGE T. SIMON

Stamford, Connecticut
April 1961

THE QUESTIONERS

Folks keep askin' me to explain 'em jazz. Guess they mus'
'spect I know what it's all about, seein' as I come from New Orleans
and once upon a time I played with the likes of King Oliver and
Louis Armstrong and Sidney Bechet and the other great men
down there.
But I ain't no big man with them fancy words. My horn does all

my 'xplainin'. I keep tellin' 'em it's the way I play that shows
'em what jazz is all about. But that don't satisfy some of 'em—
'specially the ones who keep tappin' their feet all outa time when
we're playin'. They want words—big, long words, like some of them
jazz writers are puttin' out with. They make good readin', I 'spect,
but to my way o' thinkin' they're most all too booky and they can't
give you none o' that free, down-to-earth feelin' that's jazz.
That's it! That's what I oughta tell 'em. Jazz is a feeling deep down
inside of you and it can make you feel real warm and mellow
or real hot and excited. Us jazz musicians, we show that feelin' in
all sortsa ways—by the way we bend a note on the trumpet, or
give that ol' trombone just a little extra slide, or the way we rough
up the tone of a clarinet and give it some more guts and sadness
both. It's how we play things—anything at all—not what we play,
that gives jazz that feeling—our feeling. It's what the right
hand is sayin' to the left hand when they're playin' ragtime or boogie-
woogie or any kinda jazz on the piano, and it's what they're both
sayin' together to the drummer. And it's that drummer man, too, as
he lays down that nice, easy, steady, rockin' beat that keeps all of us
happy and movin' along together. You know, the greatest of all jazz
feelin's is when the whole band gets the spirit at the same time and
each man knows right off that they're all playin' fine jazz together.
And the folks who are listenin'—they'll know right away too—that
is, if they got any feelin' at all for jazz. And if they don't? Well, I
guess they're the ones who keep on askin' for the same ol' explanations.
But how you gonna tell 'em what they're supposed to feel when they
can't feel it in the first place?
Reminds me of a great clarinet man we used to know back home. He
was blind, and always had been, but he sure played great blues. One
night somebody said to him, "Blind Boy, you most certainly blow
fine blues. Every time you play I can jus' see that color blue all
through the room." And Blind Boy, who'd never in his life seen any
color at all, asked the man, "What does blue look like?" And you
know, for the life of us, none of us could tell 'im. Not a one. There
jus' was no way. And it's the 'xact same thing with jazz. Jus' plain
words can't do no good.
You gotta be able to feel it.
And if you feel it, then what do you need words for?

THE
MORE
IMPORTANT
PEOPLE

There are things about jazz musicians some people just don't
understand. I don't mean the people who come to hear us play; I mean
the more important people, those we're closest to—our families.
Our way of life is different and it makes theirs different, and if we're
going to remain jazz musicians there just isn't much anybody can do
about the situation. Take me.

I've got a family but it's a family I don't really know. Worst of all,
they hardly know me, and I have a feeling sometimes they don't even
trust me. Take Rachel. She's a good wife and a good mother. She
comes from a good Christian family that always went to church
regularly. She never knew or cared about the music business before
she met me. She still doesn't. "Honey, when we get married," she

used to say, "honey, you can settle yourself down in a good job, a respectable job, and you'll come home regular-like and I'll have dinner waitin' for you and we'll raise a family and we'll all be happy because we'll all have each other, just like it was planned."

Well, I guess maybe I thought I could go along with the plan, and yet deep down in my heart I knew all the time I could never give up playing jazz. Still, after we got married I did try a regular daytime job—several of them—but I could see that none of them had a future for me like jazz. Maybe if I'd been born white, it might have been a little different. Anyway, I picked up my horn again and started practicing, which almost drove Rachel crazy, and soon I was back in jazz, playing regularly, six nights a week. I was happy and making good money once more, and before long we had us a good home and a family. But what we didn't have, I found out, was a real family life. When I worked in town I'd be gone until three or four in the morning at least, and I wouldn't get up till around noon.

Well, Rachel stood it for a while, but then folks started talking and asking her things like "Are you sure he's really working all the time?" and I could feel her cooling off even though, believe me, all I've ever done after work is go out and grab a bite and maybe a drink with the guys or maybe bowl a couple of games at one of those all-night alleys—just to relax, you know. After all, a man gets pretty wound up playing jazz and it's hard to slow down quick, just like that, and come right home to a house that's still and go right off to sleep. You have to unwind first. But how do you explain that to someone who doesn't understand jazz and maybe doesn't even understand you? I love Rachel, and I think she knows it, but I find it's getting harder and harder for me to reach her. And as for my two great kids, it's pitiful. Lately I've been on the road so much I hardly know them and they hardly know me. And I don't know what I can do about it, either, because a band can't play in the same spot all the time, you know. Yes, I guess *you* might know, but *they* don't. They want a daddy like their friends' daddies, a daddy who comes home every night and plays with them and tells them stories before they go to bed. And even when the band's in town and I'm home at the house, they can't understand why I have to pick up my horn and practice to keep my lip in shape. They keep looking at me like to them I'm only a trombone player and not a real daddy. Believe me, that hurts, but what can I do?

As I said earlier, there are things about us jazz musicians that are different. And some people just don't understand.

THE SESSION

Aw, c'mon, Bill. You gotta make it, man. . . . No, it ain't like last week. I mean it. It's a swingin' thing this time and they're all tellin' me to ask you to bring your horn. . . . Naw, you're outa your head. Nothin' like that. I said it ain't like las' time. Nobody's tryin' to cut nobody else. . . . I know. . . . No, he ain't here tonight. I'm tellin' you, Bill, there's no prima donnas. We all feel like playin'. Nobody's tryin' to prove anything. It's a real groove. . . . Who? . . . Hell, no, he ain't here either. Who wants him? . . . No, Joe's here. He's playin' drums, and you know Joe, he's always playin' for you, not against you. It's a real soft groove, believe me, Bill. . . . What's that? Juice? . . . If you wanna, but who the hell needs to get juiced tonight. . . . Sure, we had a couple but that's all. . . . Yeah, there's one jug here, but nobody's killin' it. We're feelin' sociable. I'm tellin' ya, Bill, it's a swingin' thing. . . . Who? . . . Yeah, I know 'er. Sure, bring 'er. She digs. That's another thing, Bill, this time we got nobody lookin' in to see what a jam session looks like. Nobody's askin' us to play nothin'. We're just playin' what we feel like. . . . Why didn't we let you know sooner? How the hell could we? We didn't know ourselves. Me and Herm jus' happened to be working out some changes we'd been wonderin' about and Bert and Joe started listenin' and pickin' up and before we knew it we had a session goin'. . . . Naw, Bill, he's no problem. He's here listenin'. He digs. He said he'll keep the joint open for us as long as we want. He used to play, remember. Maybe we'll even have him sit in a number to keep him happy. . . . I'm tellin' ya, Bill, this is a real swingin' thing. . . . How many times do I have to keep hippin' ya this ain't like last week. Nobody's tryin' to be a hero. We're friends. That's why they asked me to call you. . . . That's right. . . . O' course. . . . I keep tellin' ya, Bill, this is a special thing. It's relaxed and groovy. We all feel like blowin'. . . . How's that? . . . Crazy. See you in a little while. . . . Only make it quicker!

THE CREAM

I wonder if it ever occurs to those supercilious snobs how rudely they are behaving. And, if it does, whether they care.
I see spread in front of me—or, peculiarly enough, below me—what is supposedly quote, the Smart Set, unquote—the superbly educated and immaculately reared who have inherited the social standing and

the financial wherewithal entitling them to a ringside seat in a delightfully intimate and frighteningly expensive night club that features jazz—not, I'm certain, because it wants to attract jazz-lovers or give jazz musicians an opportunity of being heard in an attractive room, but rather because some consider it darling that jazz has been brought up out of the gutter and so chic to come to see and hear some of its species in person.

Perhaps I shouldn't feel so bitter because, after all, I am working regularly with a good jazz group, I am able to stay here in town with my family, and I am being paid a respectable salary. True, we are limited to playing almost exclusively show tunes in a swinging and straightforward way, but when we're off the stand I sometimes sit down and talk and drink with some stimulating people. But just as often I'm apt to be set upon by a table of condescending, well-heeled and equally well-liquored boors, who, I have a feeling never offer me a drink because they're confused and embarrassed by a well-educated and quote, different, unquote, Negro, and who don't know what to do or say because I don't fit into their stereotyped impression of a colored musician, and so they just talk awkwardly to me about jazz and brazenly suggest I play some of the real jazz classics like "When the Saints Come Marching In" or "Muskrat Ramble" or some numbers equally unsuited for the piano and as tradition-bound and as two-dimensional as their own minds. On the other hand, perhaps if I did acquiesce, they might pay more attention to the music and merely clap their hands on the wrong beat instead of trying to shout over us.

And yet I wonder. I can't see that there is anything, including our fulfillment of requests, or the most money and the highest social standing in their register, that can compensate for such an innate lack of social graces and sensitivity of feeling for fellow human beings, whether they be black, yellow or white—or blue-blooded. For this peculiar species of our society seems to come here for two purposes: to be seen and to be heard, and I must confess, the more they are heard, the less we are. Sometimes we even try playing double pianissimo to try to shame them into social submission, but such subtleties don't seem to affect them at all.

Here's what really gets me: if this is the cream of the social strata that made it so difficult to complete my education—to gain admission to a first-rate college, to attend a musical conservatory, and finally to secure my appointment to the faculty of a nonsegregated university—if this is the cream, then, brother, all I can say is please keep on serving me my coffee black!

THE
KING
OF HAPPINESS

You askin' me am I havin' a ball?

Damn right I am!

I love what I'm doin'. I been playin' this boogie-woogie piano for I dunno how many years, and believe me, mister, you ain't the first customer come up to me and ask, "Big Bill, you still havin' a ball playin' the same kinda piano ever' single night?" You know what? I always got me the same answer. "Mister," I says, "Big Bill don't never get tired when he's playin' boogie-woogie 'cause boogie-woogie is Big Bill and Big Bill is happy bein' hisself."

Yes sir, this is 'xactly what I always wanted. Even when I jus' started in growin' and we had an ol' beat-up Victrola 'round the house, I useta latch on to all the boogie-woogie records I could lay my hands on— them old ones by Jimmy Yancey and Pine Top Smith, and later when I grew up some I'd keep on listenin' to them things by Pete Johnson and Albert Ammons and Meade Lux Lewis. I'd play 'em and close my eyes and think 'bout the tales my Auntie Flo useta tell me 'bout them rent parties they had out in Chicago and how them boogie-woogie pianists would play right through till eight in the mornin' without ever stoppin' and everybody'd be havin' hisself and herself a real ball. Yes sir, ever since I can remember I been diggin' that boogie-woogie, with them poundin' eight beats to the bar in the left hand and the tremolo and the shakes and the hard-drivin' trumpet-soundin' things they was makin' with their right hand.

I remember too how I useta sit me down at the piano over in my auntie's house—I musta lived there, it seems—and I'd figure me out how they was doin' all those things, and then gradual-like I began to make it.

I never had no formal trainin'.

Nobody never gave me no lessons.

But I had that feelin' inside. I knew that hard, drivin', steady beat
was for me. I could almost hear it say, "Billy Boy, help me get outside
from inside o' you and together we'll make the whole world sound
real happy." And that's 'xactly what did happen, and it's been
happenin' ever since.
Oh, sure, I know some folks say, "Bill, with your talent you oughta
be doin' more'n just playin' the same ol' boogie-woogie in some ol'
night clubs. You could do lots more, like Erroll Garner who never
took piano lessons neither, or like Mary Lou Williams who made all
them great boogie-woogie records with Andy Kirk's band and is now
playin' real pretty and modern. Why you jus' wanna stay here for?"
Mister, if you ask me, them questions are jus' plain stupid. They don't
know what real happiness is like. I'm livin' precisely like I want to,
doin' what I want to—so why should I change? Playin' boogie-woogie
always makes me feel good. It's got a rhythm and an excitement I
don't hear in no other kind o' jazz. It's the blues, 'cept it's not sad
blues. It's a happy blues, if you get what I mean. And if it makes me
happy, and if it makes all the folks who come hear me play happy—
and I know it mus' make 'em feel good or why else would they come
hear me in the first place?—if it makes everybody in my world happy,
why should I be the one to try to change things? If I tried to do all
the other things folks are suggestin', if I tried to make it like Erroll
or Mary Lou and tried to do all them fancy things that I don't feel
or know nothin' 'bout—if I tried bein' somebody else instead of bein'
me—you know, I could wind up bein' a real joker and I'd be makin'
nobody happy—least of all me.
No, when I'm playin' boogie-woogie I feel like I'm the King—and
ain't nothin' and nobody is gonna take that
feelin' away from me!

KID STUFF

Listen to what they're playin'. That's kid
stuff. These young modern guys, they
don't know. They got no idea of what jazz
is all about.

> They got ideas—lots of ideas. They're full
> of 'em. In fact, that's what they got most
> of—ideas.

Maybe 'bout some things—but not about
jazz. They got no sense of time. They got
no feeling. Listen to that damn drummer,
all over the place fillin' in, but no time at
all. Rushin' like all hell. That stuff ain't
got a beat, and if it ain't got a beat, it
ain't jazz.

> Right. But they'll tell you they got a beat.
> What's that word they use? Oh, yeah—
> "implied." They claim they got their own
> special "implied" beat.

Like maybe it's here and maybe it ain't.
What sorta guff is that? There's no maybe's in jazz. You gotta know for sure. You
gotta be damn certain you feel somethin',
not just imagine you do. If you got a beat
to lay down, then lay it down, but don't go
pussyfootin' around with it hopin' maybe
somebody's gonna catch on to what you're
thinkin' and maybe get the message. The
beat's gotta be right in there. That's what
makes jazz hot.

> That's not what they think. They got dif-
> ferent ideas. They like to play it cool—
> just like their whole generation.

Progressive vs. Dixieland

But that cool stuff ain't jazz. It's more like that classical shit. Let's face it. When you play jazz you feel like sayin' somethin', or even shoutin' it out, but you sure as hell don't feel like whisperin'—and whisperin' in riddles, at that.

Maybe they're too inhibited to shout.

Inhibited, hell. They don't feel nothin' in the first place. Listen to their sound. It's small and weak. Reminds me of a baby that was always suckin' water instead of milk out of its bottle and never had a chance to develop. It's thin and it's got no guts and no color like real jazz has gotta have. You know, when you blow a trumpet or any kind of a horn the right way, it sounds round and smooth and warm like —well, you know what I'm thinkin' of.

I'm hip.

And then you change from that mellow sound and you get that real live and angry and edgy sound, like you almost want to kill the thing you was just lovin' so well just a second ago. Take the way Muggsy Spanier or Wild Bill Davison or Buck Clayton or Cootie Williams or any of them blow—it's not dull-sounding like you want to apologize for playin' jazz—like you might be ashamed of it. It's got guts and emotion and it says, "Look, here I am and I'm glad I'm livin' and I just wanna blow and blow and blow!" It's like a man who really knows who he is and what he wants and where he's goin'!

But most of those kids don't feel like that. They don't know who they are or what they want or where they're going.

Then they oughta find out before they start playin' jazz and tryin' to tell the world this is it, when they don't even know what "it" is. They oughta listen to more guys like Louis, who they're always puttin' down, or Teagarden or Hawkins who could blow any of 'em right off the stand. Just listen to that thin, puritanical, snob-sounding tone that alto's makin'. All those fancy notes and runs, they don't mean nothin'. They got no feelin', and without feelin' how you gonna reach people?

Who says they're tryin' to reach people? They just want to reach themselves, and to hell with the rest of the world.

Then I say to hell with them. Jazz has got to be a ball for everybody—the guys who play it and the guys who listen.

You kiddin'? They don't even know what havin' a ball is like. They're so wrapped up inside themselves, they can't let go.

That's my point. If you can't let go, you
can't play jazz.

But they say they're playing it. The sign
outside says they are. The critics say they
are. And all the kids who buy their records
—I don't mean the teen-agers, I mean the
college kids—they all say it's jazz.

I don't care what they say or the sign says
or what anybody else says. I'm tellin' you
this ain't jazz—and I oughta know 'cause
I been playin' it all my life—and from
here, right from the heart.

They don't care about that heart stuff.
They want to show the world they're bright
young kids and they know their music inside out. That's how they get jazz kicks—
thinking.

Then they must be sick. Look, you know
damn well when you think too much about
somethin'—when you just think and think
and think—it don't take long before you
lose all feelin' about it. You think it to
death, and when you find that feelin' is all
gone there's no amount of thinkin' is
gonna bring it back. Maybe if you relax
awhile and just let go, then you got a
chance to feel somethin' again. And that's
how I feel about jazz. You don't fight it or
beat it to death. You just let it be, and
there it is—your friend. But, as I said,
once you start thinkin' too much about it
and keepin' it all inside, and worryin'
about this little thing and that little thing,
tryin' to figure out in your head all the
whys and whats and hows of jazz instead of
just acceptin' the fact that you got a feelin'
for it and thankin' God that you can blow
it out your horn—once you start thinkin'
and doubtin' that way, you're dead. And,
believe me, so's your jazz.

OLD MAN STUFF

You mean those are the cats who've been putting us down? Just listen to 'em. They've been playing the same old tired things since the year One. They'll never change.

> They couldn't if they tried. And talkin' about changing—they've been making those same chord changes since the original saints came marching in.

What else can they do? What else do they know? They huff and they puff and then they all look at each other real happy and satisfied-like—like they just made the greatest scene of all time. Look at them!

> I see them. But don't try to tell me anybody can really be that happy. They must be putting it on.

No, they're not. I know. I once played a gig with them. That's their natural style. They're happy in their own little world, doing what they've been doing for years, taking no chances, playing the same thing night after night and telling themselves they're having a ball.

You mean you made that scene for a whole night? Man, I would've gone out of my skull. That's strictly for old men.

Well, take a look at who's playing it. Look at that drummer, pounding out the same steady monotonous beat—even on his bass drum—the same naked beat they've been using for years. Makes 'em all feel secure, I guess. All the horns have to do is go along for the ride. Nobody worries. Nobody thinks. Nobody cares. What's that they like to call it? Emotional jazz.

Like emotions can excuse everything, even no brains and no control. Like a guy murders somebody and he comes up before the judge and he says, "Sorry, judge, I got all emotional and excited. I wasn't thinkin'." And the judge says, "Oh, that's okay. You're a great Dixieland musician and when you get emotional you don't know what you're doing. Case dismissed."

That's a hip judge. But, seriously, I pity them. I mean, like you know, how can you go through life never changing? Never moving ahead? Never even interested enough to see what's around the next corner? At least we're looking and listening and trying. We don't want to settle for the same dreary old sounds, playing the same old tunes in the same old way, living in the glories of the past.

Glories, hell. What's so glorious about stomping around the bandstand and dreaming you're marching down Bourbon Street or else closing your eyes and squeezing your horn and trying to remember what Louis Armstrong felt like when he was playing in some dive on Chicago's South Side. Maybe when you get to be in your forties, yes. But me, I'm young and I want to live and experiment—even if I do make a few hundred mistakes. But at least I want to try.

Try what?

Well, like you know what, man. New things, like Bird did and like Lennie Tristano and Thelonious Monk and even Ornette Coleman, though between you and me I'm not sure I know exactly what Ornette is making.

That's not important. I know what you mean. At least he's trying. He's trying new rhythms and new sounds and new harmonies and new about everything. And that's a hundred times better than never trying anything new. I bet you I can hum in advance every note that trumpeter over there is going to play.

That's not hard. Look how few he plays.

Yeah, but to quote those guys, "It's not so much what we play as how we play." That's what keeps dragging me—the fact that they just can't understand it's the "what" that makes the difference between dull jazz and interesting jazz. They're too involved with making sensuous sounds with all those vibratos and slides and slurs and playing what they call their emotional jazz and then hoping somebody will dig and share their so-called emotions. To me jazz has grown up beyond that. You don't need all those tricks any more. It's become more like a science. And so you think before you play, and if you get something interesting to say, you just go ahead and say it without all that fancy business. You say it straight. Then people will dig you for what you're saying instead of how you're trying to say it. Between you and me, I'd rather play one important and original thing that maybe just one guy will dig—even if it's just a guy in the band— than have to repeat over and over again what a million other musicians said before me, and probably much better, too. I don't want to make excitement. I want to make music. And if I can't blow forward, then, man, I don't want to blow at all!

SWING

Man, I'm glad they said to take five, because this next arrangement looks rough. What a range! And what crazy intervals! And in the key of B natural at that! Now I know what Al meant when he phoned and said, "Look, they asked for you special on this date. They're tryin' for a new kind of sound-gimmick record and they need a first trumpet that can read fast and get around his horn and still have the feeling of jazz."

Well, I guess I ought to feel complimented, even though I know I'll be bleeding and sucking wind by the time it's over. But, let's see: this date'll bring me up to over four hundred dollars so far this week, and this is only Thursday morning. Not bad for a kid who was making seventy-five a week during the swing era— that is, when he wasn't being kicked around from band to band because he couldn't read well enough. "Look, boy," they used to tell me, "you play great jazz but you're lousing up our section. Why don't you learn to read and study your horn some more?" At first I wouldn't listen because I'd been believing all those romantic tales about how none of the great jazz stars could read music. But then, after I'd been kicked out of enough bands and also found out my idols, like Bunny Berigan and Harry James and Peewee Irwin, were fine readers, I came to my senses. I studied hard, finally got a job with Dorsey, and from him and a couple of other musicians I also learned the more subtle things about playing in a big band: how to blend with the other horns, how to match my vibrato with the others, how to shade, how to use the various

TRAINING

mutes correctly. "Remember, kid," they used to reassure me, "you
don't have to give up playing good jazz just because you know
how to read and get the most out of your horn. And nobody's
asking you to play stiff or mickey mouse like Lombardo's or
Welk's guys. What you have to understand and accept is that what
arrangers are writing for swing bands is jazz also, even though it's
something you didn't create. It's the arranger's conception.
It's his ideas which he's creating just like any jazz soloist. But
instead of playing them on a single horn he's writing them down
for all of us to play. We're his horns. We're playing his jazz."
And one more thing they pointed out to me: "The easier you
find it to read, the easier it'll be for you to relax and blow the
written notes with a jazz feeling, the way the arranger originally
heard them in his mind before he wrote them down."
I soon discovered they were right, that knowing your horn
and knowing your music and knowing all the ways of getting a
certain sound or reaching a certain note more easily—that all
those things don't detract from your ability to create your own
jazz. They only make it that much easier for you. That's why
today, even though I don't get to do it as much as I used to, I can
blow jazz just as good as when I was a kid—probably even
better, because I know my chords and my horn better.
Meanwhile I'm also able to make a good living, to support a
healthy and happy family by playing all kinds of studio dates.
Sure, some are big drags. But others, like this one, are exciting
and a challenge as well. And you almost always get a chance
to play with some great musicians, and most of them came
out of the big swing bands.
That's one thing you've got to hand that era: it taught you
how to be an all-around musician instead of just a soloist. But
with so few big bands around these days, I wonder about the
future of today's kids, especially the ones who blow only that
far-out stuff in their own special way and with their own
uncontrollable sounds; the ones who look down on us because
we're willing, and also able, to play commercial dates, dates
they couldn't possibly play because they don't have the
equipment or the experience. I wonder how they're going to
make a living out of music when they're our age.
I'm sure glad somebody taught me the facts of life in time.

ME AND MY HORN AND NOTHING ELSE

Well, here I am. I made it. I wonder what Dad's gonna think
now. He tried but he couldn't stop me. I can still hear him.
"Son, you better give up those notions of yours. That jazz is no
good. It's downright evil. You talk about going to New York
and making a career for yourself, but I'm telling you, son,
I'm not about to let you do it. I know all about what that jazz
music does; how it makes folks wild and do things they oughtn't
be doing, and how it leads to drunkenness and dope addiction.
Why don't you get serious about your music instead of fooling
around like you do? Stay here in town and join the symphony
orchestra and meet the right sort of people. You can work with
me in the store and on nights when you have a concert to play
I'll let you off early. But put that jazz music out of your head,
son. It can mean your ruination." . . . Well, here I am—without
Dad's blessings and with Mom's tears. It's my first time in
New York, and it looks awfully big, but I know I can make
it—if I can find somebody to hear me. . . . Dad always said not
to be too cocky, but he and Mom could never understand that
there's nothing makes me feel so strong, so much like a man,
as playing my horn, blowing what I want to blow and how I want
to blow it without anybody or anything except maybe the
chords, telling me what to do. But how could they understand
when they'd never even listen to jazz? "No boy of seventeen,"
they kept telling me, "really knows what to do." But they're
so wrong. Maybe I didn't make the greatest grades in school,
but when it comes to jazz I *know* I know what to do. It's
not only what I know in my head about music and about my
horn; it's what I know and what I feel in my heart. Other guys
may be happiest when they're playing ball or rebuilding a car
or dating some chick, but for me it's always been jazz and my
horn and nothing else. So here we are, me and my horn and
nothing else. . . . Now what do I do?

"YOU KNOW WHAT

WE'RE LOOKIN' FOR"

I feel like pushin' somebody's face in!
Who the hell do they think we are, makin' us come down
here to be fingerprinted, like any lousy criminal, so we can
get a card that lets us work in a night club.
If that isn't typical! See a musician and right away you see a
junkie. No questions asked. You're a musician so you're guilty
as hell until you can prove yourself innocent. That's how
they all think.
I'll never forget the time I was on a band and the leader was
so clean-living and decent we didn't even feel like cussing when
he was around. He didn't smoke and he didn't drink. But what
happens? We're in a car after a job and some trooper spots
our horns and drums in the back seat and the next thing we
know he's wailing his siren at us. Then he orders us to pull over
and get out of the car, and he takes this poor leader guy and
makes him stand up against some wall with his hands raised over
his head while he searches him from head to foot. When the
leader asks him what it's all about, he sneers. "You're
musicians. You know what we're lookin' for." Naturally he
found nothing and so he had to let us go.
Did he apologize? Like hell he did! He gave us a warning
instead: "Just get on your way and keep out of trouble."
Now what sort of way was that to act! "You know what we're
lookin' for." And "Keep out of trouble." And all we should
have done I suppose is bow meekly and say "Yes sir" and
"Thank you Mr. State Trooper for not arresting us for doing
nothing." When the devil are some of those Boy Scouts going to
stop tryin' to be heroes and make newspaper headlines at our
expense?
And that's another thing. If the press would stop all that
sensational crap about us, maybe the attitude of the cops might
change too. How many times do you see some stupid gossip

columnist make a nasty, lying crack about musicians and drink
and dope. They may be easing off on other minorities, but not
on us. Always a little dig here and a little dig there. And the
same goes for some of those idiots who write novels about jazz
musicians. They don't know the first thing about the jazz so they
cover up by writing all about drink and dope and sex as if
that's all we live for. But why pick on us all the time, when
there's more boozing and cheating going on among writers and
advertising men and their snooty suburban housewives than
you'll ever find among musicians. And if the police are really
looking for somebody to line up against a wall on a cold winter
night to search for junk, why not try a doctor or a nurse?
Let them make a thorough study and see what group does have
the highest rate of narcotics users. But, for Christ sake, let
them lay off us for a while, all of them: the police, the press,
and all the rest. Let them stop trying to turn the world against us.
Sure, if one of us does something wrong, arrest him. And put
any junkies they find away some place to be cured. But then
when they are cured, don't keep on hounding them merely
because they happen to be jazz musicians! Don't stop them
from making an honest living by holding back their working
permits.
I know of one good, clean musician who's led a hell of a rough
life because he was convicted on a narcotics charge when he was
a kid in college. He was cured. But you know, it took him
almost ten years before they'd allow him to work here. Ten
years, even though the law itself had docked him for less
than one.
And now here they are, fingerprinting all of us, hoping maybe
they'll dig up another poor fool who might have gotten
himself into a jam and who has paid his debt to society but
whose life they'll make so miserable that they'll drive him right
back to using the stuff so they can pick him up again. That's
what makes us so bitter: their hounding and hounding us just
because we're jazz musicians; their always suspecting us; their
always considering us guilty until we can prove ourselves
innocent. Is this the price we have to pay to live and work as
jazz musicians in our society?
If so, maybe we'd all be better off playing nothing but Irish reels.

ME

I'm a very lucky fat girl.

I'm not pretty.

I don't have a mint stashed away.

I don't even have a husband any more. I had one once, a long time ago, but he must've grown tired of me or the life I was leadin' or somethin' and so he cut out.

I couldn't blame him. There's lots prettier chicks around.

But I've been livin'. I've been livin' the way I like it, doin' what I want to do. Nobody's been tellin' me how to run my life and, best of all, nobody's been tellin' me how to sing. Nobody ever had to.

That's where I've been luckiest. From the time I was a young kid I just felt it, and out it came. Oh, sure, I learned the fundamentals. I sang in the church choir and I paid attention when they taught us how to breathe and how to use our voices right. But from then on I sang the way I liked, and I guess I was lucky, because it seems I always could find somebody who wanted to hear me.

For awhile I felt like singing with bands, and so I sang with bands. When radio came along I had my own show, and I had a ball, coast to coast. I've always liked making records and I guess if they ever make television screens wide enough they'll be inviting me to fill them up more often. I can't think back and say I have any regrets, because in all those years I've sung

with the same feeling and the same beat and the same
natural way that I guess you can say is just me.
I've been very lucky in a bigger way, too, because the good
Lord's always let me be honest with myself, and it's never hurt.
Many times people have tried telling me I should be more
commercial. I shouldn't sing all those jazz songs, they say. But
I've never quite understood them because to me there is no
such thing as a jazz song. Any song can be a jazz song,
depending on how you sing it. I've sung hundreds of the same
songs other singers, the so-called pop singers, have sung.
They've sung them straight, just as they were written, and I've
sung them with a jazz phrasing and a beat, just the way I felt them.
That's the only difference.
And I'm not saying my way is better than theirs. All I'm
saying is that my way makes me feel better.
And, what's more, I'm not at all jealous because some of them
are so much more popular than I am. Because I don't believe any
of them—Dinah with her TV shows, Doris with her movies,
or Joni with her records—have what I've got. Remember:
they've always got to please everybody.
But with me it's different. I've got only one person to please.
Me.
And, thank goodness, so long as I can keep on doin' what
I'm doin', I've got the easiest job I know.

THE LAW OF THE

Look at him. There he goes again—honking, squealing,
stomping his feet, weaving back and forth, putting on another
of his shows. And listen to those lunkheads screaming at
him. It makes me want to throw up.
If that isn't a new low in jazz! Imagine taking a great artist
like him and throwing him to those howling wolves. He never
did those things before he joined us. Even on his first few
concerts he just stood still and relaxed and blew the same
beautiful lyric style he always did. And he gassed us up on the
stand. It was a privilege just being on the same stage with
him. But the audiences? They kept sitting on their hands until
another tenor man everybody knows can't blow in the same
league with this guy comes honking on stage and cutting him.
Not as a musician, of course, but as an exhibitionist, as a typical
jazz-concert show-off.
Well, it didn't take this guy long to dig the scene. He knew
if he didn't make the customers scream he'd be through with
us, through with making the really big loot that only big-scale
jazz circuses like this can pay.
So he gave in.
He changed his style and he changed his stance, and before you
know it he's honking and squealing and hitting high notes that
make no sense and stomping his feet and going through the
whole ridiculous routine. And he's killing the audiences—
those great jazz-lovers who come to clap their hands on the
down beat and stamp their feet on no beat, and whistle, and go
through the whole idiotic scene.
Only with them it comes natural.
But for this poor guy it's only an act he knows he's got to go
through, so he won't be cut by this other cat who comes tearing
out of the wings, squealing and stomping and making noises and
faces and striking poses I know he doesn't believe in
either—but who learned earlier to respect the law of the loot.
And I know all about this other cat, too.
I should.
That's me.

LOOT

THE IMPOSSIBLE

They'll never make it. I knew pretty well what was going to happen when I started to do this thing; but, no, the maestro kept insisting his musicians were good musicians—"excellent players," he kept calling them—and they could "perform with distinction" any music set before them, including "your jazz music."

Well, I did the best I could. I didn't write anything too far out,

just middle-of-the-road swing, all ensemble with a few simple
riffs that would be extremely easy for any musician with a
feeling for jazz to play. What's more, I also wrote down the
precise tempo at which the arrangement would swing most, and
wherever possible I also indicated the manner of phrasing.
After all, if a symphony pops orchestra decides it wants to show
the rest of the world how well it can play "Lullaby of Birdland,"
it behooves us jazz players to give it all the help we can.
But all the help won't be enough. Just listen to how they're
phrasing that figure! A little while ago I suggested to them
how they might play it, and they all gazed toward me very
politely with one of those "and to whom the hell in the name of
Wolfgang Amadeus Mozart do you think you are talking" looks.
Obviously, though, they didn't understand, because nothing
I said could get them to loosen their phrasing and their attack.
I knew the two old geezers behind the drums over there
couldn't help them any with their Civil War beat, so I tried the
old Glenn Miller rehearsal approach—having the horns play
their parts without any rhythm instruments—hoping they'd be
able to feel the beat and the right phrasing themselves. But,
except for one clarinet and one trombone player who'd played
in dance bands before, all of them gave it the old beer-garden
approach: everything right on the beat, exactly the way it was
written, magnificently stiff and stolid like a beautifully trained
Prussian regiment.
Finally their concertmaster took me aside and said, "Look,
young fellow, if you wish us to perform your music the way you
want it to be performed, write it precisely as you wish us to
play it. After all, you must realize that we are, unlike many of
you jazz musicians, accomplished readers, and we are able to take
direction expertly." That's when I tried explaining to him
that in jazz the nuances are so minute and so subtle that it's
impossible to write them down. Even if you broke down the
notes into one-hundred-and-twenty-eighth notes or even
five-hundred-and-twelfth notes and wrote directions for
phrasing each fractional part of each note, the result would still
be stiff and unjazzlike unless the musicians lost their formal
approach, relaxed, and let themselves feel the music.
I suggested the best way to understand and to feel was to
approach it freely without prejudice. "But, my young man,"

he replied, "we know no prejudice. We play every kind of music written, Russian, Italian, German, French, and American as well. You must remember, we are all excellently trained musicians of the highest reputation."

Well, I could see he was beginning to take all this as a personal insult, so I walked away without bothering to point out to him that mere excellence of training cannot of itself guarantee excellence of interpretation of every form of music, and that musicians so deeply steeped in classical traditions and in the over-all philosophy, or perhaps psychology, of musical dependence upon a conductor or maestro of some sort might not be able to accept the free feeling of individual initiative and personal creation that are absolutely essential to the playing of jazz. I was even going to bring up the analogy of the enemy flyers in World War II—especially the Germans, who had been superbly trained in group movements; but they lost to the Americans because our men had always been instilled with a feeling of personal freedom, and could adapt themselves more spontaneously, and could fly extemporaneously when necessary, and could even ad lib just the way we do in jazz.

It is, in a sense, all part of the same thing, this feeling of freedom in jazz and in our American culture. It's a reflection of two entirely different approaches to life, which has been obvious to those of us who work in the studios where time and again you'll find the string players and a few other non-jazz-orientated musicians acting and reacting so differently from the jazz men. For some reason or other they seem to need and to want strong discipline and leadership, while we jazz musicians neither need it nor want it. As in Erich Fromm's book, *Escape from Freedom*, they do seem to want to escape *from* freedom, while we are trying to escape *to* freedom. And so long as these diametrically opposed attitudes do persist, experiments such as this one here are doomed to failure.

Oh, yes, you can be reasonably certain the orchestra will receive a large ovation when it finishes playing this arrangement tonight, but not so much for excellence as for effort, not so much for the jazz as for the novelty. For they're trying to do exactly what I predicted when I was given this assignment—they're trying to do the impossible. And from a jazz point of view, I must say they're failing admirably.

THE
REG'LAR
LIFE

I hope Bill's not gonna leave.
I don't think he should. It'd be all wrong. He belongs here and I love
him, not only for myself but even more for himself, and I don't think
he'll be happy where he might be goin'.

Sure, it must be a big temptation when Lionel Hampton himself calls
long distance on the phone—and not collect—and tells Bill he wants
him to come join his band. But Bill, he's had them kind of offers
before—not from such a big band maybe, but he's had leaders in
New York and Chicago and Detroit callin' him and sayin' things like
"Bill Hopkins, man, you come on up here and we're gonna make you
a star. What you wanna stay down there for, wastin' your time in one
of them territory bands where you know you're never gonna make
no real money? Man, you're abusin' your talents, that's what you
are. Come on up here and really start livin', man!" And every time
they call, Bill comes to me and we sit down and talk things over, and
I keep remindin' him 'bout the times I went up to New York and then
up to Detroit to sing with some bands and how lonely and unhappy
I was and how different it all was from bein' down home here where
we been livin' all our lives and where we don't have to keep worryin'
'bout everybody tryin' to cut us down to size so they can step over us.
I told him too 'bout the musicians I met up there, and how they'd been
happy playin' with territory bands like him and how they were
moanin' and groanin' 'bout havin' come on up and that it just wasn't
the same good feelin' like back home. It was more like a business,
they said, and businesses don't have no good feelin'—in fact, they
have no feelin' at all—period.
Sure, of course, sometimes some o' them men got feelin' good for
awhile, 'specially if the bands they were on got makin' a gang o'
records and settlin' down in some spot like Birdland and the leader
happened to like what the individual musician was makin' and givin'
him plenty of action. But too many times it turned out a man was
a hero one minute and a bum the next, and I keep on tellin' Bill he's
much better off bein' a hero all the time right here. That's what
most men don't understand. They should thank the good Lord for

what they got, 'stead of always tryin' for just that little bit more.
And Bill, he's always said he's happy with what he's doin'—in fact
he keeps insistin' there's more good honest jazz being played reg'lar
in bands like this than you'll find in most of the big name bands.
That's something folks everywhere don't seem to know about. We
got some wild swingin' bands spread out all over this land of ours—
bands that nobody 'cept the folks in their particular territory ever
get a chance to hear, or even hear about. That's how it's always been
and how it'll always be. Remember,
Basie was a territory band before John Hammond brought him to
New York, and the Jimmie Lunceford band did lots of scufflin' 'round
Ohio before it hit the big time. But there are still plenty of bands like
this one we got here that've been swingin' this way for a long time now.
And we play great jazz, too. We got the feelin' all right, and we can
play relaxed and groovy and swingin' all the time 'cause we're not
havin' to worry 'bout that some manager or some big-time night-club
boss or some man from some recordin' company is gonna try to tell us
what to do and how to do it. I tell you, we may not get the same
attention some of the big bands get, but we also don't get the same
tension, if you know what I mean. We can live a relaxed life, a reg'lar
life, where the food is reg'lar and your friends are reg'lar and the lovin'
is reg'lar, and the jazz, of course, is reg'lar as well.
And that's what Bill appreciates. I know for sure he can't stand none
o' that tension. He's an artist, and I know it, 'cause nobody can make
me sing like he can when he plays those pretty riffs in back o' me.
Sure, I know everyone else can hear them too, but he keeps tellin'
me they're just for me 'cause that's how I make him feel, and I believe
him. It's the most tender and the most wonderful sound I ever heard,
and I'm aimin' to keep it right here, near to me for ever and ever. . . .
No, I don't think Bill's gonna leave.

ANOTHER ORDINARY MUSICIAN

Jeez, I wish I could go to sleep! But I can't. I can't get that phone call out o' my mind. . . . Poor kid. Poor Bobby. . . . And me not able to do a goddam thing about it. . . . Who ever heard of a seven-year-old boy needing a hernia operation! And to think he's gotta go in a ward, like a charity case, just because his old man turned out to be a no-good bum runnin' around the country, playin' in a band and never makin' enough loot to take care of his kids like they should be taken care of. . . . Christ, last time, when Cindy took sick, I could at least borrow on my insurance. But how can a guy pay back on that when he's only pullin' in a hundred and a quarter a week? Hell, I useta be makin' four or five times that, before Madge and me even had our first kid. Of course, that's when I was the great young jazz star and the swing bands was fightin' over me and the critics ravin' about me and the kids yellin' for me and askin' me for my autograph. I believed it all too. . . . If I'd only hadn't let my wig get that big—if only I'd'a listened to that guy on the Barnet band—I can't even remember his name now—the older guy who always kept telling me I oughta learn to read right instead of half fakin' like I did, and to blow my horn like it was meant to be blown insteada showin' off like a freak all the time. But no, I figured him just another ordinary musician—no big jazz star like me—and so I'd keep puttin' him down with things like "And where did *you* finish in the *Down Beat* poll?" and go on my way like I always did. After all, who the hell needed to know how to play flute and oboe anyway? My public came to hear me blow tenor. I was makin' it and I knew I always would. . . . Christ, I musta been one cocky kid! . . . And that's just what did it. Not booze or pot but just being so goddam cocky and believin' the wrong people. I was havin' a ball every night. All the loot and kicks I wanted, and everywhere the band went everybody'd know who I was. Makes me wanna laugh—

or cry. . . . Tonight, who the hell knew who I was? Last night, who the hell knew who I was? The night before last, who the hell knew who I was? Nobody, except maybe the guys in the band, and they been comin' in and goin' out so fast I bet some o' them don't even know my name. . . . Not that I can blame 'em for cuttin' out, with all these goddam one-nighters and practic'ly livin' in this bus and eatin' lousy food and bein' paid chicken feed. Christ, I'd pull out tomorrow too if I could find somethin' else to do, somethin' that'd at least let me know where my dough was comin' from each week. . . . Never forget a few months ago when I got bugged about somethin' and one of the kids got real salty and asked, if I useta be such a great jazz hero why wasn't I playin' in some jazz band insteada this ricky-tick outfit? Now how the hell could I tell him the truth: that I was too damn scared to cut out; that I knew I couldn't make it with the young jazz kids any more; that jazz had changed and the freaks were out of style, and, besides, that all the high notes and the fire and the spirit that made me a hero twenty years ago was dead and gone. . . . Maybe they knew anyway, just like they must know I still can't read worth a damn and that I never did learn much about music and so I can't go into the studios like some of the guys I used to play with, and the only reason I'm stayin' on here is because I been with the band so long I know all the angles, so I can be the road manager and watch over everything and still cost 'em no more than just another ordinary musician. . . . That's me: another ordinary musician, playin' in a band that's got no feelin' for jazz—only for makin' loot. Christ, when you think of what it used to feel like, when all the bands were swingin' and all of us couldn't wait to get on the job each night. That was some feeling—some great feeling—standing up there and blowing and having the whole big band behind you, feeding you and making you feel like you was the President, even though you weren't old enough to vote. . . . Christ, what a come-down this is! What the hell am I doin' here and where the hell am I goin'? . . . But who the hell am I to start feelin' sorry for myself when I got little Bobby at home havin' to go into a hospital ward just because his old man didn't have the brains enough and guts enough to make somethin' of himself when he had the chance? That's who I should be thinkin' and worryin' about and feelin' sorry for. Bobby, the poor kid—what's gonna happen to him? . . . But what the hell can I do? I can't even go to sleep.

THE
UNEXPECTED

This is exciting! Something none of us expected. Funny thing, it just happened to happen because somebody goofed and called just the five of us a day too early for band rehearsal.

Nothing else to do so we decided to blow. Bass, piano, trumpet, and two alto saxes. Lousy combination for a jazz sound, and when we started I gotta admit it was a heavy and stiff and ridiculous mess.

Then Joe put away his sax and put together his clarinet. That made it a little lighter and looser.

And then Al said to me, "Mac, try the flute. Let's hear how that sounds." It was better, but still too legitimate.

Then Joe and I decided to kill our vibratos and blow straight tones and then the whole thing began to sound airier and cooler, with a jazz feel.

And then we hit on the idea of clary and flute blowing things in thirds against the trumpet making contrapuntal things in the lower register with just a light, delicate, relaxed beat from piano and bass—nothing strong, just kind of an indication of where we were going. That was it—one of those floating, swinging things, even without drums. Crazy sound, but a little hard on me because blowing so much flute is rough on your lips unless you keep at it. Tomorrow I start practicing again because I really want to get with this new thing. Guess you could say I'm inspired again. That's one of the great things about jazz. You can experiment and you can use your own imagination and you never know when you'll hit something great like this. It's different from other kinds of music, where you got hard and fast rules and it's all tradition and you're always being told you can't do this and you can't do that because this guy didn't do it this way and some other guy didn't do it that way. But in jazz you can feel free.

It reminds me of the feeling I used to get when I was a kid and the school year was over and all of a sudden it hit me that this was summer vacation and I didn't feel hemmed in any more and I could do what I wanted.

That's how I feel now.

And all because somebody goofed!

THE JAZZ-KILLERS

Why the hell don't agents and club owners try to understand what we jazz musicians are trying to do? Look at those two over there—my agent trying to talk the boss into holding me over for a coupla more weeks when he knows damn well I can't stand this joint. I keep telling him the acoustics stink, the piano's always out of tune, and the waiters keep rattling dishes all night long. "Stop thinking like a musician," he says. "Where else can I get you this kind of bread, buddy boy? Be realistic. Right now you're a hot property so let's make 'em pay you what I tell 'em you're worth. Who knows what I can get you a couple of months from now?"

I try to tell him that if he'd be less of a pig we could play in more clubs, including some that aren't run by goons like this creep here who hasn't the slightest idea of what we're doin' and who doesn't give a damn anyway. Sure, this week he's our friend; he lets us play our kind of jazz, which he obviously hates. Why does he let us do it? Simply because we're pulling in the customers and he's pulling in a pocketful of bills. But just let that change and right away he'll stop being our friend and start ordering us to play "Melancholy Baby" like Sammy Kaye. Or, who knows, he might throw out jazz altogether and put in some strippers.

Remember back in the forties when that happened on Fifty-second Street? It had been a swingin' scene in all those jazz clubs like the Onyx and the Famous Door and the Three Deuces. And everybody—

Basie, Hawkins, Dizzy, Bird, Woody and the rest—was having a ball, every night. And then what happened? The war ended and people started spending less money on entertainment. "Jazz is dead!" cried the club owners triumphantly, and they put in the cheap strippers, so right away a bunch of great jazz artists began scuffling. And the thought of the same thing happening again keeps on buggin' me. A star today, but where the hell will I be tomorrow? There aren't too many jazz joints as it is, and if some of these idiot agents keep on squeezing the clubs, and the clubs keep on milking the kids and everybody else who wants to listen to jazz, what's going to happen? That's a lot of ifs, and if so many business men weren't trying to make so many quick bucks out of jazz, we could have many more clubs for people who really want to come and listen. And they'd be steady customers, too. And think how much happier the musicians would be. I can name you a hundred guys like me who'd rather play for less money—but steady—in joints where they're really appreciated. But try selling that to some of those agents. Except for maybe a few, all they're after is that big commission—and if they don't get it from jazz, there's always some other flesh they can peddle. Maybe they don't dig jazz, but if this keeps up they'll be digging its grave, and the thought of jazz ever dying quite frankly scares the living hell out of me.

THE FORTUNE COOKIE

You know, I think this kid believes he really knows what he's doing.
And maybe he does. After all, what is he doing? It's simple: he's
playing three chords and singing out of tune and making himself
a fortune.

I can remember when I used to sing and play guitar like that long
before anybody invented rock and roll. I must have been about twelve,
and I'd heard some of those great rhythm and blues singers and
thought I'd try to do what they were doing. But it never came out
right; it always sounded like a bad imitation of good jazz. I had enough
brains or pride or something to quit. But not this kid. He won't quit.
He's got too many leeches telling him how great he is. And he
believes them.

I think he even believes what he told me a little while ago: that he's
expressing himself like any true creative jazz artist, "the same as you,
mister. Only I don't need no written music. I never did. Everything
I do comes from inside here." And he points to his heart as an excuse—
an excuse for making a mockery out of such great rhythm and blues
singers as Big Bill Broonzy and Leadbelly and Tampa Red and all
the rest who sang the same blues this rock and roll is based on—
except they sang it with feeling, with a warm and honest jazz feeling,
because they were saying something that was a part of their lives.
Oh, sure, I know, he's telling the world this is part of his life too, and
he's right. It is. Not any artistic part. Not any creative part. No, it's
the financial part, meaning his managers who tell him how to sing,
his music publisher who tells him what to sing, his booker who tells
him where to sing. And then there's his record company that makes
all his horrible tricky sound gimmicks without giving a damn about
music or what it's doing to the country. And there's his record
distributor who bribes the disc jockey to push his records into the ears
of a young public that's been weaned on this sort of maudlin, moronic,

mechanical manure and won't settle for anything better. They're all a part of him, a part of his comic-book world of music.

And so are we: the jazz musicians who can't earn a living making jazz records because the record companies tell us we play too good. But still they always call us in when they want to make a record with a cookie like this because it doesn't take *us* three hours to learn the chords to one tune and because *we* know how to keep time and don't skip beats and because *we* can hold the rest of his nitwit pals together and because, in the final analysis, *we're* professionals and *they're* not.

I suppose if anybody wants to pass judgment on us on a purely moral basis, we're just as dishonest as he is because we're sure not doing anything to help music or jazz. All we're doing is going along for the ride. It doesn't make a guy feel very good, believe me. It'd feel much better telling them all to go to hell.

But in a world like this who can afford such a luxury?

THE FREEST

Hey, this must be the band Les Brown was talking about! I heard 'em
the other night when I was passing the Officers' Club and, as Les said,
they were playing the purest schmaltz. I remember I was thinkin'
the Japs must be a little hipper than that. Now I can see they are—
much hipper! Imagine being sharp enough to play that ol' business-
man's bounce tempo so a lot of colonels can wheelbarrow their wives
around the dance floor Stork Club style and then coming down here
to a club like this and blowing this real groovy jazz!
What a crazy world!
If you want to please an American, you don't play jazz. But if you
want to please a foreigner, you do play jazz.
Ridiculous.
But it's just what Les and other musicians said after they'd come back
from overseas: the place where jazz is least appreciated is the place it
came from—America. I remember reading what Woody Herman
once said, too: the greatest audience he ever played to was the one in
Vienna. Lionel Hampton's said the same thing about Israel. And look
what happened in England. The King and Queen go ahead and ask
for Duke Ellington. But when did he play a command performance for
our President? And of course there's always Louis. Because of guys
like him and Diz and others, they're beginning to get the feeling of
jazz all over the world. And it's the freest thing we can give them.
Don't think they're not keeping up with us either. Just listen to some
of the modern things this group is making. And remember how they
dug Stan Getz in Sweden and kept him there for years. And then
there's the story of Elliot Lawrence walking down a street in Moscow
and hearing a Mulligan record coming out of a window. Even the
Russians, he found out, are starved for American jazz. Over there, in
fact all over the world except in the States, people really dig that jazz
program Willis Conover's been putting on for "The Voice of
America." Betcha that's how this tenor man here's been pickin' up
on Sonny Rollins. They even pick up on little things, like they have
a Japanese jazz critic who took the name of George Simon in honor
of some guy who used to write for *Metronome*.
Hey, a funny thing just hit me. Till now they've all been pretty much
aping us—I mean like this tenor man blows like Sonny and the
trumpeter's got a bit of Diz and Miles in him and the pianist's tryin'
to make like Bud Powell. But what a crazy gas it'd be if all of a

sudden they decided to blow their own special kind of jazz over here and they did everything strictly Oriental style using just the five-tone scale. And then along comes Ed Sullivan and he hears one of these bands and he books them on his TV show and immediately the whole scene becomes the biggest and the entire United States discovers jazz overnight and radio stations play it all day and all night. Everything's going along real great till one day some senator remembers the Japanese band on the Sullivan show and decides jazz must be foreign so naturally it's got to be unpatriotic and subversive. So they pull one of those big investigations, and they finally force jazz to go underground, which means that after all these years we're just about back where we started from.

But then the Supreme Court steps in and it decides jazz really did start in America and that it's perfectly patriotic and constitutional. And what's more, all nine judges agree unanimously that jazz musicians are first-class citizens and they should be integrated with the rest of the citizens of the United States immediately!

Hallelujah!

Hey, waiter, lemme have some more of that crazy saki, will ya? This is one dream I don't want to lose!

SPARK PLUGS AND

Who was it once said: "If you want to be a drummer but you have no beat, you should give up before you begin and become a plumber!"
I think it was Davey Tough. He should know. He *was* a drummer! But this new freak we got here. Whew! I can't imagine what kids like him are thinking about. Or don't they think? It must be obvious to him, like it is to anyone who plays jazz, that above all else you've got to have a sense of time. But this is the third drummer we've tried in a month who's all over the place, trying to show us his great technique, all his tricks, and how fast he can play, and all that jazz. Still he's got no time.
What goes through these kids' heads anyway? Do they think drums are strictly a solo instrument? Ever since jazz began everybody knows that the backbone of any band—Dixieland, swing, bop, progressive— the backbone of all of them is the drums. If the drummer can't keep time, nothing's going to happen. He's the one who's got to set us in there, the one who's got to dig that groove we can all fall into. And that means he's got to feel and think about music as a whole and not just about how he can make all kinds of fancy things that'll make some of his friends say, "Crazy, man, crazy. You're the craziest, man. You ain't like that Buddy Rich or Jo Jones, man. You get new ideas. You're talkin' with those drums, man!"
Talking, hell. Talking to who? Talking to himself, maybe. But we here in the band don't hear it.
All we're hearing is a lot of mishmash, a lot of fancy beats and tricks that mean nothing except to throw all of us off. Listen to him—fast one second and slow the next, like a car with one bad spark plug. . . .
Funny I said that. That's exactly what a drummer's got to be. He's got to be the spark plug of the band—and a damn dependable one at that. Every great jazz group's had one. Krupa with Benny. Jo with the Count. Davey with Woody. Craw with Lunceford. Buddy with Dorsey. Art with the Jazz Messengers. They were the sparks. They drove the guys with their beat and still their times was so sure they held everything together.
But this kid here, he's doing all he can to tear us apart.
I'm trying my damnedest to keep good time and still make the right chord changes with the horns, but I can't do it all alone. In jazz we all got to play together, but he won't even give you a chance.

PLUMBERS

If only those kids would learn time first and flash second,
then maybe they wouldn't frustrate
the rest of us the way they do.
Why can't they get it through their
thick young skulls that unless you have time in
jazz you have nothing at all? . . .
Hey, maybe I ought to tell him
about the plumber bit. Naw, he wouldn't make
it there either. After all, even a plumber's got to work
with somebody else, sometimes.

IN ANY MAN'S WORLD

I've been reading in the Paris editions about the latest school-integration riots they've been holding down South, and I must say I'm delighted to be here. I love my country, mind you, but that doesn't mean I have to love all the people and the things they do.

I must admit I was lucky because I never had to feel too much of that deep-seated prejudice. I was born and raised in the Midwest, and the only times I went down South was when I couldn't help myself, like the times the band I happened to be with scheduled dates down there. And then we knew it wouldn't be for long, that this wasn't our real life; and so we took things as they came, and in our own way we'd even be laughing at some of those Georgia crackers—only they'd be too stupid to catch on. In a few days we'd head back North and everything would be cool once more.

Remember, this was during the Big Band days, when we were heroes to many kids—many white kids, too—and so far as most of them went, we were musicians first and Negroes second. Of course, that held only so long as we remained musicians—on the stand or among other musicians, white and colored, or at some of those peculiarly integrated parties that were thrown for us after we'd finished playing a date—integrated because everybody except the band would be white.

But I used to accept all those things—until I returned home from here the first time. Then I knew right away I'd been kidding myself all the time; that even as a Northern Negro I'd been closing my eyes

and ears to things I knew existed but which I kept pretending didn't.
Within the circle of jazz I could see everything was still cool. But once
I stepped out of that circle, what a difference! No more of that musician
first, Negro second bit. I had to admit it: I was a Negro first and a
human being second, something I'd never felt during all my two years
in Paris.

Can you blame me for coming back?

Here everybody treats you as if all of life lay inside
the jazz circle.

Nobody thinks about your color. I have friends, just like I had
musician friends at home, who I have to think about twice before I
can even remember what color they are. Sure, they treat me with
respect because I happen to blow a pretty good horn, but even if I
didn't—if I just blew my nose—they'd still act the same. Their only
standards are the simple, over-all standards of human behavior, not
those of extraordinary musicianship.

To be more specific, I can't imagine myself sitting in a place like this
on Fifth Avenue in New York, or on Chicago's swank North Side—
let alone on Peachtree Street in Atlanta—without somebody doing a
double take. Here *they* never give it a thought, and I never give it a
thought. Which is why you'll find a number of us colored musicians
in Paris. For here we can feel free not only in a musician's world
but in a man's world—and in any man's world at that!

ONE MORE TIME?

I know what's going on in that control room. They're putting their heads together and they're saying, "Why can't these guys play this number as great as they played the last one?" Well, the answer is simple: We don't feel like it.

Not that we don't want to feel like it.

We just don't.

I bet we've gone through this thing eight or nine times but we still don't feel it. It just doesn't come off, and the harder we try, the stiffer it gets and the less it sounds like jazz. It's different than the last tune, when it all came out great from the beginning. We hit the tempo right the first time, and the horns blew the lines just like they were improvising instead of reading, and the chords lay so good it was easy to blow solo.

That's how it happens sometimes. You fall into a groove and you feel fresh and loose. And so that's how it came out. Great, for that one. But we've been reading and working and hacking through this one so many times we're getting tense and we're sounding self-conscious and not making it at all. We're pushing instead of relaxing.

These recording guys ought to know by now that in jazz you can't play the same thing over and over again, like you would some pop tune, and make it mean anything. It's the difference between creating and manufacturing. You just can't manufacture great jazz. And they shouldn't expect us to produce what they like to call "inspired spontaneity" every time we blow, especially with those mikes staring at us all the time, reminding us that every note we play is for good. Making records is a great thing, but it's still not the same as playing

in a club where you just do a thing once and if it doesn't come out exactly right nobody's going to hold it against you for the rest of your life.

I know how some record companies work. They call in some guys, give them a couple of jugs and say, "Okay, now make us some jazz records." And what happens? The same old tired and uninspired blues choruses that everybody's been doing for years.

But we're serious about this.

We feel we have something new and deeper to say and it's important to us that we make damn sure we say it exactly right so people will understand us—and respect us, too. And it must be obvious we're not saying this piece right—at least, not right now. Maybe a little later, after we've done some other things, we can come back to it and feel fresh and do it like we feel it should be done. But certainly not now. . . .

What's that? . . . They're saying, "One more time"?

Well, I sure hope they know what they're doing.

I don't.

THE REAL HEROES

Glamour?

Wha's that I keep hearin' 'bout all the time—how folks keep talkin' 'bout the glamour of jazz in the early days, how it come up nice and easy, so smooth and natural and unmolested on them ol' Mississippi riverboats.

Seems to me like I been hearin' them same tales ever'where— readin' 'bout them in books, seein' 'em in motion-picture shows, and seems like I even seen a television show too had something 'bout them so-called romantical days of jazz. I got one question to ask 'bout all this. Was any one of them writers or storytellers there to see and hear all that stuff? Was they there watchin' jazz jus' glide up nice and smooth and easy up the river and settle itself down in Chicago like it was invited? You know, I bet you none of 'em really know the real story 'bout all that was happenin'. But me, I do.

I was there.

And so was some of my pals.

And believe me, mister, jazz didn't come up or grow up in no easy way. It come up the hard way, the real hard way, like anything that's Colored has always had to come up.

Sure, I reckon it's true a good part of it begun to grow down in New Orleans where they had King Oliver and Bunk Johnson and Sidney Bechet and Jelly Roll Morton. But that ain't the only spot. There was things happenin' early in St. Louis, too, where Scott Joplin was playin' ragtime piano 'round the time Mister William McKinley was the President. And there was more things happenin' in the honky-tonks out Kansas City way—more things maybe than some folks like to talk about. And you don't hear much 'bout it today, but there was jazz in Arkansas and Mississippi and Texas and down in ol' Alabama, where I come from.

There was jazz wherever the colored folks would get together, and they didn't play it only when they was comin' home from some funeral, like some folks lead you to believe. They jus' played it whenever they felt like sayin' somethin'— when they felt like bein' free. It wasn't no cut-and-dried affair. Nobody planned nothin'. It jus' happened.

Now don't you try tell me all them musicians one day decided to pile in on some ol' riverboat and said, "Mister Skipper, anchors aweigh! We're movin' on up the river and we're gonna play all the time and ever'body along the way's gonna hear

67

our music and soon they'll all be playin' it like us." It wasn't no
single bunch a' jazz pioneers brought jazz to the rest o' the
world. Oh, yes, Oliver and Louis Armstrong and the Original
Dixieland Jazz Band, they helped in the big cities. But jazz
was also growin' up in a lotta little towns you never heard of
and bein' played by a whole gang of musicians and bands
you never heard of neither. And most of 'em done it the hard
way—the real hard way—'cause it was somethin' they wanted
to do and it was a way of makin' themselves a livin' and
they wasn't lettin' nobody stop 'em.
They never thought they was blazin' no trails neither. Again
I got to remind you I know, 'cause I was there. We had us a
band down in Mobile we called the Dixie Serenaders and we
had some real good jazz musicians with us. Other bands'd
come from miles round jus' to hear us play and for a long time
we was right content and happy. But then one day we all got
bit by the bug that tol' us to move on. So we did. We kinda
mapped out ourselves a itinerary, takin' it step by step.
Well, none of them steps had no glamour—never! It was rough
goin' all the way. We had ourselves two cars between the ten
of us, and, with all the instruments and the size they made
cars in them days, you can't say we was 'xactly travelin' in the
lap of luxury. Wha's more, anybody knows no band of
colored folks, least of all colored musicians, is gonna get
themselves much of a break from anybody down in the South.
No sense right now tellin' you 'bout all the things happened
to us, but, mister, if you wanna hear a little sermon on flea
bags and jail cells and smelly night clubs where at the end of a
week the owner refuses to pay you and says, "What'cha gonna
make of it, nigger boy?" and jus' plain sweat and stink and
lousy food and the runs—well, just ask me. I'm tellin' you, you
won't be hearin' no glamorous words.
And what was happenin' to us is the same as what was
happenin' to most of them other territory bands. Maybe we was
luckier than most of 'em, or maybe even better, 'cause we
stayed together as far north as Nashville. But when nobody'd pay
us no mind there, we jus' plain give up at last, all 'cept the
two of us—me and a trumpet player named Dillard Roberts.
Now Dillard was the greatest I ever heard, and I heard
Louis and Oliver and all the rest—and me and Dillard, we

decided to see what we could see. We'd heard there was
more gold up North, and I always knew for sure if Dillard
made it he'd take me right along with him. As I said, we was
dead broke, so I took me a job washin' dishes, and Dillard,
who was a real smart man, he went to work in a factory. Well,
you may of heard what happened to him. Poor fella. Guess
he shoulda been more careful, or maybe they shoulda been, but
anyhow he got himself cut up so bad in one of them big
machines they had to stick him in one of them colored hospitals
where they didn't have many real good doctors. I went to see
him regular and tried cheerin' him up some, but it got his
chest and he knew he'd never blow again and so he didn't care
much 'bout livin'. The doctor tol' me he died of TB, but I
know it had to be a broken heart.
Well, anyway, after workin' real hard, washin' dishes day-
times and playin' music nights, I managed to save me enough
money to go travelin' some more. I been blowin' my horn all
the time I could and I was gettin' better, so each time I got to
some town I'd look me up some colored band and sit in, and
many a time they give me some work. But it still was hard
goin' all the way and sometimes I'd get me so discouraged I
wanted to turn back and never play my horn no more.
But then other musicians began lendin' me encouragement,
'specially when they found out I knowed Dillard Roberts so good.
So after a while I started feelin' better and thinkin' maybe I
could make it. Well, as you know, I did make Chicago at
last and I got me a reg'lar gig down on the South Side, and if
you been readin' them jazz history books you know my story
from there. They got it pretty straight.
But don't let too much of that other stuff fool you. There
wasn't no glamour, you can bet on that, mister.
Go ask any of the musicians who done what I done—'specially
the ones who didn't make it as good as me. They was the
real heroes of jazz—the unsung heroes—'cause it's each and
every one of 'em—not just the few that folks always keep talkin'
'bout—who helped spread the jazz gospel. They was the ones
who took it from where it began to where it went, to where
it is now. And, you know, judgin' by what's been happenin'
since I first blew my horn fifty years ago, they all done a pretty
fine job, don't you think?

THE LOST MAN

It's hard on me too, Millie. I've been trying to do all I can
for Jim, but—well, you know as well as I do what the
trouble is. . . . No, of course not; it's not his playing. Jim can
play great any time he's in shape. Believe me, I dig him,
as a musician and as a man. You know that. Why do you think
I've been befriending him all this time? But tell me,
honestly, if I said to you right now I wanted him to open at
Basin Street tonight, would he be in condition and would
he show up? . . . What's that? You'd go out and look for him
till you found him? . . . Honest, that's very touching, and
I'm not being sarcastic either. But if you, his own wife, don't

have any idea of where he is or when he might be showing
up, how do you think I feel? . . . C'mon now, that's not fair.
I'm not just interested in the commission. Look, if it
were just the money I'd have given up on him a long time ago.
Do you think I'd have kept on giving him all those advances
when I knew right along what sort of stuff he was blowing
them on? Believe me, Millie, there are a few of us in this end
of the business who do have a heart and who do have a
feeling for jazz and who do want to do something for the
musicians we admire. Jim's always known how I've felt about
him. . . . No, please don't act like that. I'm not saying all

this because I want to hear how grateful you are. What
I'm trying to tell you is that there's a reason for my having
tried this hard for your husband. That's why I phoned you
in the first place. I'd heard he'd disappeared again and I
figured it must have been the same thing as last time. . . . No,
this time he wasn't supposed to be working any spot for us.
After what happened in April—you remember, when he
didn't show up after the second night of the gig—after that,
we figured we'd better wait and see. You know, this wasn't
the first time he'd done this to us, and some of the other
men here at the office—well, they've been sort of getting on me
and telling me to stop acting like a starry-eyed, frustrated
trombone player, which I guess I am, and to cut out what they
call this hero worship I have for Jim. . . . Yes, I'm sure you
worship him, too. . . . Of course it's even tougher on you. It must
be murder living with a thing like that. Frankly, I don't see
how you've stood it all these years. . . . No, I'm not talking
against him. . . . Yes, I know he's a wonderful man. . . . That's
right, he is just sick. But how are you going to explain that
to a night-club owner who's lost a potful of dough because Jim
didn't show up? Or to some a. and r. man when some
record comes out that Jim swore he played his greatest on,
only everybody else swears he must have been out of his skull
when he made it—which you and I know he was. No, you
know what those promoters and those record men say when you
tell them Jim was sick? "If he was really sick, then have his
doctor send us a written excuse." They don't understand
that kind of sickness. How many people do? . . . Yes, I
know. . . . You do, and I do, too. But we're a minority. . . .
Right. But isn't that the way it works so often in jazz? It's
the minorities who feel the things the most and who suffer the
most, too. But never forget this: Jim's a member of a
minority too—the most misunderstood, the most frustrated,
the most lost and the most miserable minority not only in jazz
but in the whole wide world. . . . I know. One of these
days he'll find himself. . . . But listen, Millie, instead of talking,
let's get busy and do one thing right now—the most important
thing we can do—let's find Jim!

"YOU GOTTA GO, BOY!"

Hey, I'm beginning to feel it again!
And, damn it, it's that jazz band
that's bringin' it back for me. It's a
crazy, swingin' scene! Makes me
really feel like skippin' this here rope
for the first time in I don't know
how long. Makes me feel real free and
loose—not all tightened up inside
like before that last fight. And, man,
how I stank up that joint! I tried
everythin'—talkin' to myself, singin'
out loud, even hammin' it up to try
to relax—but nothin' worked. I jus'
couldn't unwind. It was like a
little speck a' dirt got in the works
somewhere and threw my timin'
and my rhythm and
everything else
off jus' a fraction
of a second,
enough

to make a bum instead of a champ outta me. But, hey, man,
this group's got what I been needin'. I ain't skipped rope
like this in months—maybe years. They're relaxin' me. They're
gettin' me to feel that beat again. They're like sayin',
"Jackie, you jus' lay it in there nice and easy-like and we'll go
along with you. And if you start losin' that beat, if you start
tightenin' up again, you jus' listen to us 'cause we'll keep on
swingin' and we'll bring you right back into the groove."
It's a crazy thing 'bout jazz and how it can make you feel real
strong and sure of yourself. I remember before that last
fight overseas, all I heard for months while I was in trainin' was
that Latin music crap. Now that ain't for me. It does
nothin' to me at all. And as the fight was comin' up and I knew
damn well inside me that I still didn't have it, I tried puttin'
on some jazz records and I even tried loosenin' up by singin'
riffs to myself in a swingin' kinda way. I tried the best I
could, but it was too late. I was pushin' instead of relaxin' and
swingin'. I tell you for sure it wasn't nothin' like this here.
Man, what a gas: this band blowin' riffs just for me. They got
no words but I can jus' hear 'em callin' out:

> *You gotta go, boy,*
> *You gotta go, boy,*
> *You gotta go, you gotta go,*
> *You gotta go, boy!*
>
> *You gotta go, boy,*
> *You gotta go, boy,*
> *You gotta go, you gotta go,*
> *You gotta go, boy!!*

Man, how can I help goin' when I hear a swingin' riff like
that blowin' right in my ear? Makes me feel like jumpin' this
rope like I ain't felt like jumpin' it since I was a kid. Hell,
I'm relaxin' and swingin' like I used to. It's a crazy bit, a
wonderful, swingin', crazy bit! Man, I'm tellin' you, no athlete—
I don't care if he's a fighter or a ballplayer or a runner or
anything—no athlete is really gonna make it unless he can
feel that real relaxed beat, the kinda feelin' jazz gives you best
of all—the greatest goddam feeling in the whole wide world!

THOSE FLIPPANT
FANTASIES

*The lushly brilliant backgrounds are not sounds but merely
a mellifluous mélange of pale purples, deep pinks, shimmering
chartreuses and reticent reds. And as for the solos
themselves, their sleek, pirouetting excursions into flights
of the most flippant fantasy almost defy description. . . .*

So this is jazz criticism! This is supposed to tell us whether
what we are making has value and substance and meaning and
whether we have performed well or poorly.
Nonsense!
All of this is just a glob of slick vocal varnish spread as thick
as possible in order to cover up the writer's weaknesses as a
critic. I've read that passage over I don't know how many
times, and the more I read it, the more I realize I don't have
the slightest idea of what the man is saying—in fact, no
more than I think he does.
For example, what about those "lushly brilliant backgrounds"?
Do they complement the soloist or do they interfere with
what he's trying to play?
Do they give him good rhythmic support so he can move or
do they tend to bog him down?
How are they played?
And are the voicings written poorly, or could they be improved
upon, or are they something extraordinary?
You know, when you get right down to it, I don't see how the
writer, by his very own admission, can tell. He says they're
"not sounds," and if they're not sounds, then how can he hear
them? And as for the solos, maybe they do "defy
description." But do they also defy constructive criticism?
I'd like to know some things, like do the phrases flow well
and do they have a logical construction?
Do they have a swinging beat?
Are they played in tune?
And are the notes correct?
Maybe my thinking's a little petty about all this, but I'm getting
fed up as hell with so much of this guff that's supposed to
pass as jazz criticism. It always amazes me how far out some of
these writers will go to camouflage their opinions, as if
they're not quite sure of what they're saying and they're scared
stiff that some day they might be held liable to someone—
perhaps the musicians themselves—for what they've written.

The same thing holds true for some of the drivel they put
on the backs of record jackets. Ever notice how long it takes
some of those guys to get to the point of the record? And
sometimes they never get to the point at all but just ramble
on and on, spouting off opinions and bits of knowledge that
have little or nothing to do with the music. It's just like
some young uneducated musician who's trying to play modern
but who doesn't know his chords and has no real feeling
for jazz, and so he merely keeps on running scales, up and down,
up and down, without ever really saying anything at all.
Too seldom do we get really constructive criticism from writers
who know their subject and, what's just as important, who've
made it their business to try to understand what we're
trying to do. How often do you read some young critic putting
down a fine Dixieland trumpeter like, say, Maxie Kaminsky
because he doesn't blow modern enough, or some moldy
fig writer knocking somebody as great as Kai Winding for not
playing Dixieland trombone. With their preconceived prejudices
they've even gone ahead and blasted some musician not
because he doesn't do what he's doing well but because he
isn't doing what they happen to like or understand. How
stupid can you get?
And yet, how many musicians will stand up to a critic and tell
him exactly what they think about the stuff he's written?
I don't understand why they don't speak out more. Don't they
give a damn, or are they scared to challenge the so-called
power of the press?
I know, so far as I'm concerned, the next time I meet the
character who's written all about those solos with their sleek,
pirouetting excursions into flights of the most flippant
fantasy that defy description, I'm surely going to ask him to
try to explain what he means. And I won't let up on him until
I get some sort of a satisfactory explanation.
For this is one time I've really got to know.
Why? Because this time it's me he's writing about!

LOOK,
BUT
DON'T
LISTEN

So this is the gal they keep telling me is too much. Maybe
she is. But not as a singer.
I can't figure what gets into these gals—I mean the nerve and
the insensitivity they must have that lets them get on the
same stage with a bunch of great jazz musicians like this and
then take over the way they do. Maybe they don't have
many inhibitions. But don't they have any ears either? After
all, there are some basic rules of music that do apply to jazz too.
There is such a thing as pitch.
There is such a thing as proper breathing and sustaining a note.
There is such a thing as controlling your vibrato. But these
are the things in life this chick obviously never learned about.
Yet look at her. Look at that cocky attitude, like she really
believes she's singing something great.
Look at those poses and that sexy, cool look.
Look, but don't listen, because, if you're like me and a
hundred other musicians I respect, you're not going to be
able to take it. This sort of thing kind of makes a guy stop and
think for a minute because, let's face it, if a gal with so little
musical quality can make it with audiences like this, then it
might not be too long before all we musicians are going to have
to do is take some physical culture course, spread ourselves
thick with Man Tan, dress down to our shorts and, man—
we're in!

And what's that they like to say about her? "She sings with
jazz feeling." For her that's no description; it's an alibi.
Sure, maybe she does have a trace of Ella's natural beat, and
maybe she does bend a few notes like Billie used to, and
maybe she does sound hoarse and husky like Anita. But all that
doesn't automatically make a gal a great jazz singer. The
feeling of those gals was always natural. They created. They
didn't steal. And they always had something else this gal will
never have: musicianship. That means not only good intonation
and control, but it means an innate, not a phony, feeling for
jazz itself. And, if you're going to mess around with a tune, it
means knowing what you're doing, singing the right notes
in the chord instead of rushing wildly out into left field and
dragging in some far-out notes that have nothing at all to do with
the song—all just to let some fool audience or tin-eared critic
think you are a creative genius. After all, just because you
create something doesn't prove you have talent or you worked
hard. All you got to do is dig this gal's body for proof. When
you create something artistically great and solid, and create
it on the spur of the moment the way any good jazz musician has
got to do—that usually proves you've worked hard and
you've got a hell of a lot of talent. But I don't think this gal
even begins to understand what either of those
things means.

JAZZ
BY THE
NUMBERS

What the hell happened? What'd Paul
walk out like that for? What'd you say
to him, anyway?

> Nothing. Nothing much. You musicians
> are all alike. You're all thin-skinned
> prima donnas.

What are you talking about? Tell me,
what did you say to him?

> Merely relaying the clients' wishes.
> They've been back there watching him
> and they think he ought to put on more
> of a show.

So what did you do?

> All I said was, "Hey there, cat, how about
> givin' out with a little more of that crazy
> jive. How about giving it the ol' Satchmo
> try?"

Holy Christ, that's *all* you said? That's like saying to your client, "Hey, bub, how come you're not drivin' a Pierce-Arrow instead of that car you got?" Can't you guys get it through your thick, ivy-covered heads that a good jazz musician like Paul, and like Satch, too, is a creator and not just another mimeograph machine!

Wait a minute there, fella. Watch who you're talking to. Remember, you're working on our team. I hired you.

To do what?

To put on the best goddam jazz show in the history of television.

That's right. A jazz show, but not a circus. If you want one of them, drop me and get one of the Ringling brothers to play on your team.

Now, now, take it easy, fella. Remember, we're carryin' the ol' pigskin together, so let's not start trippin' over our own interference.

Interference? Hell, that's all I've been gettin' ever since I started this damn thing. First they go out and book twice as many guys on the show as I said we could use, so now nobody's got time enough to create any kind of a jazz feeling. Just on and off. The next thing I hear one of your agency jerks says we oughta have some sort of a story line to hold the viewers' attention—something about a musician who's in love with a gal.

Yes, but we killed that right away, didn't we?

Sure—not because it took away from the jazz, but because some other big brain figured if you had a musician in love with a gal you might get complaints from a lot of mothers and PTAs.

Well, you don't expect us to go out looking for controversy, do you?

Oh, hell, no. That'd be asking too much. I suppose that's why you guys then insisted on an all Dixieland jazz show— nothing modern or liberal—all traditional and conservative, Ivy League, button-down jazz.

Right, that's real jazz. And it's been time-tested and proven safe. But the sponsor wouldn't buy it.

I know all about it. His kids kept insisting on the top forty tunes.

And so did he.

Yeah, until nine out of the ten acts said they'd walk off the show.

I still think the idea had commercial merit. And you'd have had no troubles with the client.

But, for Christ sake, why have a jazz show in the first place? You can't ask guys like these to play that top forty crap. They're artists, not mechanics. You can't order them to go ahead and do this and do that and expect them to create something great for you. It'd be like commissioning Picasso to paint a picture for you, only thing is, he's forced to use one of those paint-by-the-numbers things you picked out for him ahead of time.

Ahead of time, you say? Fella, you just opened your mouth and ran right smack into your interference, just like I warned you.

What in the world are you trying to say?

You talk about picking out things ahead of time. If you and your musicians had planned ahead of time, we could have saved our client a mint of money.

And how's that?

Simply by pre-recording the whole show. We could have had one day for sound in a cheap recording studio, and then we'd have had to use only one day of camera rehearsal instead of two like we're doing. But no, your musicians wouldn't or couldn't learn their music ahead of time so we could synchronize the pictures and sound.

What the hell are you talking about, anyhow? They know their music. Look, what are you guys after, a jazz show or a hit parade? Let's get this straight. You hired me for two reasons: because I've done pretty well as a TV producer and because

I used to be a jazz musician. You kept
insisting you wanted a real live jazz show.
What was that slogan you invented? Oh,
yes. "America's liveliest car presents
America's liveliest art." The only difference is, jazz can't be manufactured on
an assembly line, ahead of time, like one
of your client's cars. And another thing:
there's no mold for jazz musicians. That's
why no two jazz musicians in the world
sound alike, and no two jazz performances are ever exactly alike. And certainly
no self-respecting jazz musician will go
ahead and purposely imitate or steal from
another, the way you just asked Paul to do.

But this is show business, fella. I know
you guys live up in the clouds with your
halos 'round your heads. But if you're
never going to lift those heads out of the
huddle and run off some razzle-dazzle
plays, how do you expect to get all those
spectators in all those grandstands all
over the country to rise up and cheer for
you? And, fella, it's those cheers, those
ratings, that we're after. And you should
be, too.

Not if it means selling our souls.

Souls—soaps—cigars—cars—they're all
the same. Fella, the way to get ahead in
this world is to sell—sell anything, but
sell it good. That's all we're asking you
to do.

That's ALL?

That's all. Why? Isn't that enough?

I'm sorry. I give up. Don't ask me. Go
ask Paul. You'll probably find him somewhere under one of your grandstands,
throwing up!

A SWINGIN'

Thank you, Dodie, and thank you, folks.
You know, I'm not much good at making speeches. I mean,
I'm just a drummer. But I do feel I want to say a couple of words
because—well—you know, when something like this
happens, when somebody wonderful like Dodie stops the show
and has them bring on a cake especially for me like this
here—well then, I don't know—it kind of makes a guy feel
like he should say something. And so I guess I will.
I mean, what I want to say is these have been wonderful years
I've spent with Dodie. Just hearing her sing every night has
taught me that in jazz you can't get too much of a good thing.
Right? And it's taught me something else which makes
me feel good. I mean, what I've learned is you can have just as
much fun—maybe even more fun—working with a star
instead of trying to be one yourself.
Maybe I'm not making myself too clear, but what I mean to
say is this. Before I joined Dodie I was what I guess you'd call
strictly a big-band drummer. I made a lot of noise and it
wasn't always my fault because some of the brass sections I
played with, they came on pretty strong and a guy has to
defend himself, don't he? But I was also playing a gang of solos,
and they used to put the spotlight on me and people used to
notice me and cheer me on, and I guess I thought I was a
pretty big man.
But then one night something happened that changed all that.
Dodie's drummer took sick and she asked me would I please sit in
with her group. I gotta admit I was scared for the first coupla
sets and I guess I played pretty heavy, didn't I, Dodie?
Right? But then I started getting the swing of it, and all of a
sudden, instead of tryin' to drive a big band, layin' on top
cymbals with my sticks and workin' too damn hard to
hold everything together—instead of all that, I found myself
starting to relax and to play nice and easy, just swishing

ROLLS ROYCE

back and forth, gently and real loose with my brushes. And
when Dodie invited me a few weeks later to play regularly for
her, well, it was then I really began to live—and I been
living ever since.

First of all, I found myself playing with three sensitive people,
Dodie, Elroy over there at the piano, and Steve here on bass.
We all listened to what the other three were making, all the time.
You know, from that day on I never again had to fight to be
heard, and I never again cared about becoming a star.
And something else happened too: I proved to myself what
great drummers like Big Sid Catlett and Jo Jones and Davey
Tough used to tell me. You can swing just as great, maybe even
greater, when you play soft, 'cause the greatest kicks come
to you when you play with the least effort. You know, I wish
more people would understand that about jazz. I don't
mean so much you people who listen to it. I mean the guys that
play it. You know, folks, I can just sit here for hours, making
light, soft, swinging sounds, feeling so good and relaxed I
can't begin to describe it right. About all I can say is it's like
being part of a Rolls Royce engine that's purring along
so softly and smoothly and surely, except this is an engine with
a beautiful soul and with the swingin'est beat there
ever was.

A couple of minutes ago Dodie was saying she was grateful
for my having been with her these years, but all I can say is,
Dodie, I can't ever thank you enough for having shown me
the way. I just wish every guy in the world who plays jazz
could experience the same feeling, because, believe me, if they
did, the whole world of jazz would be the happiest place to
live in.

And now that I've had my say, folks, I'm going back to where I
belong so you can listen to somebody who's really got
something to say.

You know what's bothering me? Well, two things. One is
the way some of my jazz-musician friends keep putting me down
for coming here to study classical music, and the other is the
way some of these so-called serious musicians here at school keep
looking down their noses at me. When I tell them I'm here
because I want to learn all I can about my profession, both give
me that "come on, get off it" look, but for different reasons.
The jazz musicians seem to think that if I study music seriously
and learn all about classical composers and what they like to
call "that far-out stuff," then I'll be thinking too much
while I'm playing and nothing will sound spontaneous. They're
scared I'll become so rigid and self-conscious and bound by
tradition that I'll lose my feeling for jazz altogether. And yet
on the other hand, some of the classical musicians here seem to
feel it's ridiculous for me to be in their school in the first
place because I'm not steeped enough in their traditional
approach to playing, and, what's more, no jazz musician could
possibly appreciate the seriousness and depth of their music.
Now please don't get me wrong. I'm not saying all my
jazz-musician friends and all the classicists here have those
attitudes. But enough of them have to make me realize
that there must be thousands of other musicians in this world
whose minds are just as tightly shut and who'd benefit
tremendously if they'd learn more about music and about the
humanities in general.
What they're lacking in the first place—and this must apply
to so many people in other fields—is a willingness to open
their ears and at least try to understand what somebody else is
doing instead of always hiding behind tradition. In jazz this
goes for many of the Dixieland and New Orleans fans and
musicians who'll argue with great conviction, but little logic,
that swing and bop and progressive jazz aren't jazz at all.
They're just as tradition-bound as the most stubborn classicists
who won't admit that jazz is even music. They're all musical
reactionaries.
But maybe I shouldn't put them down too much because for
many years I wouldn't be caught dead listening to classical
music. It was jazz and nothing else. But then one day something

MUSICIAN

happened to me that happened to many other jazz musicians,
something that changed our lives and eventually helped to
change jazz altogether. I was drafted into the Army.
Not that the Army itself isn't steeped in tradition. But in the
service I was thrown together with musicians of all kinds,
because when they put together an Army band they don't practice
musical segregation. Well, what happened to me must have
happened to loads of other jazz musicians. We used to talk a lot
with other guys in the band about the kind of music they
liked and played, and after a while some of us got interested in
other things and began to listen. I'll never forget one crazy
night when three of us, who were probably the wildest cats in
the whole outfit, sat in a barracks room for hours, absolutely
bug-eared, listening to four guys playing some modern
woodwind music! We had a ball, and after that the more we listened to
various kinds of classical music, the more we began to
realize that there could be something more in jazz, something
beyond the limits of the swing and Dixieland we'd been playing
right along.
After the war, of course, many musicians who ordinarily
couldn't have afforded to go to conservatories or other music
schools took advantage of the G.I. Bill of Rights, and I think it's
because so many of us learned so much in those schools
that big changes began to take place in jazz from the mid-forties
on. Also the fact that so many musicians tried to adapt
classical forms to jazz, rather than becoming classical
musicians themselves, proves the point that once you've become
a jazz musician, once you have the feeling, you're not likely to
want to do anything else. And that, of course, is the basis
for today's third-stream kind of jazz.
But to get down to specifics, what intrigued me most at the time
was the modern classicists' contention that all music doesn't
have to be written or played in predetermined forms. When I
was blowing, I'd always thought and felt in terms of four- or
eight-bar phrases, because that's how jazz had always been. But
as I studied and listened more I began to realize I could blow
all sorts of new and exciting things if I'd be willing to think in
longer and less even phrases. What's more, this seemed

like the perfect answer to the complaints I used to hear—and
still do hear—that jazz is too limited and monotonous.

Along the same lines we also began to think how we could do new
things with rhythms. What Stravinsky and Bartók had done
fascinated us. If they could alter rhythms as much as they
did, why couldn't we, who as jazz musicians had always been so
concerned with rhythm, at least give it a try? After all, for
half a century all of us jazz musicians had been playing nothing
but a steady four beats to the bar.

So we began to experiment, but right away we ran into trouble
because we couldn't get any of the feeling of jazz into our
playing unless we stuck to the kind of a beat that had become a
part of us. We knew we had to break with tradition. But just
knowing it solved nothing. We felt self-conscious instead of free.
We couldn't relax, and without relaxation there's no jazz. But
very gradually, after we began to understand exactly what
we were doing, and after we played around with the various
polyrhythms for a long time, they began to come to us
more naturally, and so we began to feel and sound freer and
a bit more relaxed. You can get an idea of what we were
trying to do—only a thousand times better—if you'll listen
to some of Dave Brubeck's records and see how, for example,
he and the bass will be playing in three-four time while
the drummer goes in four-four. Maybe this won't seem like jazz
to you at first, but if you'll give it a chance and don't fight it,
you'll find it swings too. Or you can try groups like the
Modern Jazz Quartet or Charlie Mingus's, who'll even combine
six-four time with four-four and make it swing.

Understanding, and most of all feeling, this sort of thing isn't easy.
But no change is. I know I resisted it a long time before I'd accept
it as jazz, and it took me even longer than that before it began to feel
really right. But now I'm used to it, and I feel relaxed and swinging
both when I'm playing in the usual four-four groove or when we're
making more complicated things.

Still, I'm not completely satisfied, and that's why I'm back here at
school. I want to understand modern harmonies as well and have
them come so naturally to me that I'll be able to use them just the way I
use modern rhythms. Till now, any chords except the simple diatonic
ones everyone always learns when he starts studying harmony always
confused me. For a long time I kept resisting and failing to
appreciate Lester Young's completely revolutionary tenor-sax style.
And then after that I used to rebel against bop because the harmonies
jarred me so much. It sounded stiff and contrived and unemotional
and unmusical, and except for a handful of men who played it

naturally, like Charlie Parker and Dizzy Gillespie, I think I'll always feel that way about it. But still it must have served its purpose because it seemed to have opened a lot of guys' ears.

What opened mine was when I heard some groups using advanced harmonies and still retaining the basic, relaxed jazz beat—Gerry Mulligan, for example, and then Stan Getz and Miles Davis and a few others. Since then I've been trying to figure out why they've been able to play their advanced or extended or whatever-you-want-to-call-them harmonies and still swing, while so many other so-called jazz musicians sound as if they're just going through a bunch of exercises. And I've come up with two theories.

One is that they have mastered the concept of new harmonies so completely that these now come naturally to them. When they blow a modern solo, they don't have to consider each note carefully before they play it. Instead, they all flow out naturally, and so they've been able to retain the same wonderful, free jazz feeling that other great musicians, like Goodman and Armstrong and Teagarden, have always had playing the familiar chords. It goes back to my previous point: if you're forced to think self-consciously about everything you do in jazz before you do it, you're not going to be able to relax, and if you can't relax, you can't swing.

My other theory—and this one seems to me to be every bit as basic— is that musicians like Lester and Gerry and Stan and Miles already had a highly developed jazz feeling before they ever started experimenting with extended harmonies. And, on the other hand, it's precisely because so many of today's younger musicians have never experienced that basic feeling of jazz—a feeling that will never die—that so much of what they are now playing actually doesn't qualify as jazz at all. It's too bad, because, you know, the majority of them refuse to listen to the great jazz creators of the past—to Louis or Bix or Pee Wee Russell, or even to Jelly Roll Morton, old-fashioned as he may seem today. So, actually, they've never experienced the emotional impact, the down-home, earthy, funky feeling that's such an integral part of all jazz. Their closing their souls to what has preceded them in jazz is just as bad as some of the older jazz musicians' closing their minds to what's happening now. To the older ones jazz remains merely an emotional outpouring; to the younger ones it has become merely an intellectual display.

As I see it, the perfect jazz musician is a highly developed human being, emotionally and intellectually. He feels all jazz and he understands all music. And so he is able to express through his jazz spontaneously, emotionally, intelligently and convincingly the culmination of all his musical and personal experiences. Sometime in the future such a perfect jazz musician may come along.

About the Author

GEORGE T. SIMON *is among the best-known men in the world of jazz and will go down in its history as one of the few critics and commentators who have won the lasting respect and confidence of musicians. He was for twenty years the editor of* Metronome, *the bible of the jazz business. He has written hundreds of magazine articles and reviews of jazz performances and people. Many recordings have been produced under his direction; he has also been a producer of the most successful jazz spectaculars on television. He is currently executive director of the National Academy of the Recording Arts and Sciences, and jazz commentator for the New York* Herald Tribune.

About the Artist

Followers of jazz may well know Tracy Sugarman's style from a number of record jackets he has done. He is a free-lance artist whose work is also familiar to readers of many of the country's largest magazines. His drawings have appeared in McCall's, Collier's, Esquire *and others—as well as on CBS's television program* "Lamp unto My Feet." *He received his B.F.A. from the College of Fine Arts at Syracuse University and later studied at the Brooklyn Museum Art School and at the Silvermine Guild of Artists. He works and lives in Westport, Connecticut, with his wife and two children.*